Original title:
Jade Plant Journals

Copyright © 2025 Creative Arts Management OÜ
All rights reserved.

Author: Franklin Stone
ISBN HARDBACK: 978-1-80581-766-6
ISBN PAPERBACK: 978-1-80581-293-7
ISBN EBOOK: 978-1-80581-766-6

Light through the Leaves

Sunshine sparkles on green tips,
Little hands dance with eager grips.
Leaves wave like they own the show,
Beneath them, my wild thoughts flow.

Pot's not a hat, but I wore it so,
Plant's giggles echo—'Hey, let's go!'
Water drips like dripping jokes,
Thirsty roots whisper silly pokes.

Echoes from the Soil

Down below, a party brews,
Worms in tuxedos, sipping brews.
Tiny ferns gossip with flair,
Soil's got stories, but do we care?

Sprinkle some crumbs, let laughter roll,
What do plants eat? Some good old soul!
Dirt becomes a grand buffet,
Guests in pots are here to stay.

Life Beyond the Window

Through glass panes, the world does sing,
Birds throw parties, what a fling!
Raindrops knock like rude guests late,
While my plant rolls with fate's own weight.

Shadows dance on painted walls,
Plant joins in with its leafy calls.
Sill's a stage for play and jest,
Best friends linger, no need for rest.

Nature's Quiet Companion

In my space, a leafy prank,
Cheeky vibes from a muted flank.
A nudge today—a leaf's sly wink,
Who knew silence could make me think?

Sitting still, my buddy grins,
No judgement here, just wins and spins.
Chatting softly with my friend,
Who knew green could have such trend?

Embracing Nature's Echo

In a pot, a green throne waits,
Where I chat with my leafy mates.
They nod in style, oh so sly,
I swear they wink, I don't know why.

They dance with dust and sunlit beams,
Plotting world domination dreams.
With each sprout, they look so proud,
I blink and laugh; they're my little crowd.

The Soothing Symphony of Leaves

When the wind blows, they gossip loud,
Creating music, oh so proud.
Rustling whispers, tales they weave,
About my cooking, I believe.

Each leaf a note, a quirky tune,
Swaying gently beneath the moon.
I can't cook much, but that's okay,
At least my plants enjoy the play.

Roots and Reflections

Mirrors show the plants I keep,
Growing big while I lose sleep.
I water them; they roll their eyes,
But with my care, they surely rise.

Our roots entwined beneath the soil,
I think they plot while I do toil.
They whisper secrets, greenery wise,
Should I bring them chips? What a surprise!

Green Giants in Miniature

These giants sit upon my shelf,
I swear they're plotting to be elves.
"Mossy magic," they say with grace,
"Let's turn this room into a space!"

With every sprout, they laugh and cheer,
"Wrap us in tinsel, bring us cheer!"
Tiny rulers of my domain,
In their green kingdom, we're all insane.

The Language of Leaf and Soil

In the pot, a chatter starts,
Leaves gossip with roots and parts.
With a nod, they stretch and sway,
Ears perk up, what do they say?

Worms wiggle, worms wiggle, inside the dirt,
They're writing poems, no need for a shirt!
In this garden party, we laugh with glee,
Who knew plants had such good company?

Potted Words

Potted plants with big ideas,
Grow secret tales that bring us cheers.
The cactus pricks at life's tough side,
While ferns float dreams, never to hide.

A succulent whispers, "Life's a slice,"
"Just add some sun, and it'll suffice!"
In clay and soil, wisdom grows,
Who knew plants had such high prose?

Growing Thoughts

In the sun, ideas sprout,
Each thought a leaf, without a doubt.
Dirt and laughter mixed with care,
Let's plant our hopes, if we dare!

The watering can spills a joke or two,
While busy bees hum the tune anew.
With each new sprout, a chuckle flows,
In this green world, anything goes!

Flora's Embrace

Embraced by leaves, I dance and spin,
A wild tango with my green kin.
Petals tickle with a funny jest,
Nature's humor is truly the best.

So join the sway, let laughter bloom,
In this vibrant, plant-filled room.
With every shake, a witticism,
Embracing flora, it's our rhythm!

Tending to the Green Soul

They say plants have spirit and soul,
Tend to them well, and they'll make you whole.
A sprout who sings in the morning light,
Brings silly smiles, and pure delight.

With each little leaf, a tale is spun,
Water and sunshine, oh, what fun!
In our quirky garden, joy takes hold,
Nature's antics want to be retold!

Tendrils of Ambiance

In a pot, they wiggle and dance,
Green fingers reaching for a chance.
Each leaf a hat upon a head,
Whispering secrets, softly said.

Watering woes, a splash too much,
Many debates with their subtle touch.
Fighting dust, they rise and sway,
Making trouble, brightening the day.

Musings in the Green Light

A leaf asked me, 'Why do I shine?'
I shrugged and said, 'It's your design!'
Do you think I'll grow far and wide?
'Nah, just here, on this cozy ride.'

Pot-bound dreams with nowhere to go,
I told them, 'Feel free to put on a show!'
They giggled softly, 'Oh, we will!'
With each new sprout, they flaunt their skill.

Growth Beyond the Surface

Roots underground, plotting their scheme,
'Let's surprise them!' says a leaf in a dream.
With a wink, they stretch for the sun,
Saying, 'Watch out world, we're just getting fun!'

Neighbors peep, what a curious sight,
Wrinkled leaves in a tacky delight.
Some say they're charming, others just tease,
Yet smiles bloom ever so sweetly with ease.

A Tapestry of Leaves

In shades of green, they host a ball,
With a rustling sound, they play and call.
Some flip upside down, making a fuss,
While others just chill, fair enough, no rush!

So grab a seat, and take a break,
Watch the chaos, the joy they make.
In this leafy realm of merry glee,
Every day's a new comedy!

Boulders in the Soil

I planted hope, with soil and toil,
But my green thumb seems to just uncoil.
The neighbor's dog, my secret foe,
Found my plant, thought it was a show!

I water dreams, then watch them fade,
With every sprout, a wild parade.
The sun's a friend, but sometimes hot,
My plant just rolls—it's in a pot!

Growing Memories

Each leaf a tale, each root a laugh,
My plant's more sassy than a giraffe!
Yesterday's rain, today's despair,
I might just need a hailstorm break!

Pruned some leaves, they flew away,
I'm now the gossip of the day!
With tiny pots and pots so big,
Each watering feels like a pig!

Serene Succulence

In the corner sits my leafy mate,
Winking at me, 'Dude, I'm great!'
I talk to it, it talks back—
But only through the silence crack!

Sunshine kisses; it's like a spa,
While I sip tea, it's living la!
Its plumpness makes me laugh aloud,
A succulent that's quite the crowd.

Stories of the Verdant Heart

In whispers soft, tales grow so bright,
A plump green heart, wrapped up tight.
Sneaky squirrels eye my stash,
But it's my plant that makes a splash!

Each new leaf, a nod and wink,
"Hey buddy, how about a drink?"
A potpourri of joy and mirth,
A green giggle in this brown earth!

Flourishing in Silence

In my pot, the green one sighs,
Living life without a prize.
It grew an inch, or maybe two,
Yet all it gets is morning dew.

I talk to it, a leafy friend,
It nods and smiles, or so pretend.
Its leaves are bright, a dazzling hue,
But still, it won't share its secret brew.

Each day I water, hum a tune,
Yet all it does is soak and prune.
I'm quite convinced it's quite a tease,
Laughing softly in the breeze.

Maybe one day, it'll spill the lot,
On how it grows without a thought.
Until then, I'll just play along,
With my silent sprout, we are quite strong!

A Journey through the Leafy World

I set off on my leafy quest,
To find the plant that's truly best.
Each stem I met, each leaf and sprout,
Spoke tales that left me filled with doubt.

One plant wore hats, another shoes,
One even gave me gardening blues.
They all had secrets tucked away,
Yet none revealed a thing today!

The ferns just laughed, the cacti chuckled,
While succulents softly snickered and huddled.
They said, "Oh human, what's the rush?"
"Chill like us — don't make a fuss!"

As I returned, my pot was bare,
But laughter echoed in the air.
My leafy friends, though small and shy,
Taught me to giggle, oh my, oh my!

Green Whispers of Resilience

In my little pot, so green and bright,
A leaf once whispered late at night.
It boasted tales of times so grand,
Of winds and storms it'd bravely withstand.

With roots so strong beneath the soil,
It laughed at all my watering toil.
"You think you help? I'm in control!"
I chuckled back, "You're quite the soul!"

A little sprout, with dreams to grow,
Faces the sun with sweet, soft glow.
While I tend to it, with love and glee,
It teases me, "I'm wild and free!"

Its laughter dances in the air,
Resilient heart with a leafy flair.
So here we stand, both full of cheer,
Who knew that plants could bring such near?

Secrets of the Silent Sprout

Oh, the secrets that you keep,
In the soil where you softly sleep.
A sprout so small, so full of grace,
What wisdom lies beneath your face?

I water you, I sing and dance,
Yet you just sit, and never prance.
What do you know that keeps you mute?
A hidden truth, or a root dispute?

In sunlit corners, you bask and beam,
While I try hard to chase a dream.
Your silent giggles leave me turned,
For all this time, I've loudly yearned.

Perhaps you're plotting with your kin,
To sprout a world where life begins.
So here's my vow, I'll wait and see,
One day you'll spill your secret glee!

A Succulent's Soliloquy

In a pot so snug and tight,
I ponder life, my leaves in sight.
Do I need sunlight, or is that a myth?
For now, I just enjoy my pith.

My buddies say they need a drink,
But all I want is time to think.
Water me, please, just a few drops,
Or I might grow horns like a cactus tops!

Each morning brings me a new view,
Like the squirrel who wears shoes of blue.
I dream of fame, a meme for the folks,
With captions laughing at my leafy jokes.

So here I sit, a little green sage,
Plotting my plan to steal the stage.
Nothing's better than a carefree glance,
At life where succulents like to dance!

Nature's Fleeting Moments

Living here, my time is brief,
Counting days like fallen leaf.
One moment bright, then dull and gray,
What do weeds have to say today?

The sunshine tickles, like a tease,
While clouds move in, oh where's the breeze?
In a pot on my windowsill,
I'm learning patience, it's quite a thrill.

Ants march by like a tiny parade,
Do they know I'm just a leafy shade?
I giggle at their daily grind,
Nature's antics can be quite blind!

Seasons spin like a waltz so fine,
With growth like a well-aged wine.
A sprinkle here, a nibble there,
As I plot my vibrant gardening affair!

Walls of Green Memories

Here I stand, a loyal friend,
Listening to stories that never end.
Each leaf a tale, from spring to fall,
Giggles hidden 'neath my leafy sprawl.

Photosynthesis, my daily grind,
Transforming light — it's one of a kind.
Yet still I wonder, as I bask in sun,
What mischief lies in this garden run?

Lizards wink, while bees dance by,
With the breeze that whispers a lullaby.
Together we share this wondrous place,
A wall of green, a happy face.

Moments wrapped in a leafy hug,
Every tickle from the soil feels snug.
I'll keep these secrets, buried so deep,
As nature's kingdom rocks us to sleep!

Cultivating Serenity in Leaves

Life is simple when you're green,
Counting raindrops like a routine.
Each sprout a giggle waiting to grow,
In this cozy cradle that I know.

Meditation on a sunny day,
While bugs come to visit, tempting play.
"Don't munch on me!" I call in jest,
I'd rather be a salad than a snack for the best!

Sunbeams paint my morning dreams,
As I sway with the garden's schemes.
A leaf or two, just for show,
In this merry dance of grow and glow.

With every poke of the gentle breeze,
I chuckle softly, at life's unease.
In my pot, I find sweet calm,
My leafy laughter, a soothing balm!

Ferns of Introspection

In the corner, ferns grow tall,
Whispering secrets, yet not at all.
Counting leaves like time on a clock,
Chasing dust bunnies, a real funny shock.

Sunlight dances on their fronds,
Casting shadows like quirky wands.
They gossip with pots, oh what a scene,
Moss is the gossip, if you know what I mean!

Bored in their silence, they all aspire,
To become the life of the shader's choir.
They sway and wiggle, a plant ballet,
Yet fail to realize it's my turn to play.

One day I'll write their memoirs right,
Of ferns in wigs and a wild fright.
With stories of growth and leaves that gleam,
You'll find them chuckling, lost in a dream.

Green Memories in Bloom

A sprout in the pot is quite the prank,
Seeds whisper jokes as they sit and thank.
For every inch of sky they chase,
They plot elaborate races in their green space.

Laughter echoes through the potted glade,
As roots twist and turn like a wacky parade.
Photogenic leaves bask in the sun,
While shy little soil bugs just have fun.

Water dripping, a splatter and splash,
Turns all the plants into a sprightly bash.
They giggle at pruning, "Oh, what a shave!"
Trying to look cute, but all they do is misbehave!

Green memories bloom in pots of cheer,
Plant trophies stacked up year after year.
With wild stories of growth and grace,
Life's a hoot when it's a leaf race!

The Soul of a Leaf

In the heart of the garden, leaves take flight,
Dancing in breezes, oh what a sight!
Each vein is a story; each color's a laugh,
As sunlight tickles, they take a warm bath.

A leaf's sole purpose? To shine and please,
Yet in its spare time, it also just sees.
Photosynthesis parties never stop,
With chlorophyll grooves and an organics hop.

A leaf told a tale of a bird's wild cry,
About daring to float and learning to fly.
I swear it chuckled at the cat's swift leap,
"Oh look at that stalker, it thinks I'm a sheep!"

In whispered rustles, they keep their pride,
With roots that live in places far and wide.
Defying decay with each vibrant turn,
Leaves jest with the world, for laughter they yearn.

Resilience in Green Form

They say a cactus wears a crown of quirks,
With needles for hair, and a chubby smirk.
Yet under that armor, a heart beats bold,
In the desert sun, its story unfolds.

Succulents pose with a swaggering stance,
"Watch us survive, give us a chance!"
With just a bit of water and a ray,
They throw a party that lasts all day.

Tales of survival in pots decorate,
All the mishaps, both small and great.
"Did we mention we never complain?
In a parched world, we're the reigning champs of rain!"

Oh, resilience gleams in their leafy show,
With nods to their buddies, in gratitude they grow.
In their green journey, they laugh and they thrive,
Turning all odds into comedy alive!

The Keeper of Green Dreams

In a pot of soil, bright and lush,
A green giant waits, no need to rush.
His leaves, a sign of my daily cheer,
But they mock my watering, too near!

When friends come o'er, I proudly brag,
About my plant, they call it a hag!
Yet every leaf, a tale to tell,
Of my klutziness, in growing well.

A dance of sunlight, on every leaf,
As I share my garden, amid the grief.
I chuckle as they wilt, just a tease,
My green friend thrives, while they all freeze!

With every sprout, a laughter born,
In this home of green, I'm never forlorn.
So here's to plants, my trusty crew,
In this leafy chaos, I bloom anew.

Sunlight and Shadows

The sun streams in, a glorious beam,
But now my plant's starting to scream.
It leans so far, like it's in a race,
I laugh out loud—what's with this space?

In afternoon light, it stretches high,
I swear it's dancing, oh my, oh my!
It wiggles and giggles, don't be so shy,
Just you wait 'til night, oh how it'll lie!

My friend in green steals the spotlight,
As my other plants just sulk in spite.
They're jealous of his gleeful array,
While I just chuckle, come what may!

So every shadow, a story to make,
A comedy show that never will break.
With sunlight play, and a wink from me,
My living comedy, wild and free.

Roots of Reflection

Deep in the soil, roots twist and turn,
Secrets are held that I long to learn.
They whisper softly, 'We're not all you,'
'We make the dirt dance; it's what we do!'

Pulling at weeds, I find some surprise,
A dandelion's sneer, right before my eyes.
The roots below giggle, while I complain,
This gardening life's a comical game!

As I dig deeper, I tumble outside,
My plant just laughs, can't hold it in pride.
'Look at your skill, a true green thumb,'
While I wipe my face, dirt's so much fun!

Yet every root, like a story we weave,
In this garden of laughter, I learn and believe.
That even in chaos, joy will bloom,
With roots intertwining, life's never gloom.

Serpent Spine Secrets

The curvy leaves twist like a tale,
A serpent spine dancing, without fail.
It sways and jives, with every breeze,
But spills my secrets, oh what a tease!

Watched by many, my green little twist,
Whispers of laughter, I can't resist.
'Care for me more!' it seems to shout,
While I just chuckle, let's take a route!

So here's to the giggles, and green delight,
In the heart of my home, brought to light.
These serpent secrets, so wild and free,
With every mishap, we grow with glee!

In this wobbly garden, humor takes flight,
As I duel with leaves, a wrestling fight.
Together we thrive in this joyful scheme,
My clever companion, keeper of dreams.

Stems of Solace

In the corner, green clown joy,
Wobbly stems, my pride and my toy.
Leaves whisper tales of a sunny spree,
Spawned from neglect, it giggles with glee.

Watering can, a knight in disguise,
Raining down blessings, oh how it flies!
A sip too much, and it'll start to weep,
Yet bounce back strong, with roots that leap.

Sunbeams dance on its plump little cheeks,
Each leaf a secret, it barely speaks.
I chat with it nightly, we share all the tea,
Essential advice: Just grow and be free!

Oh, how it teases, its growth on the rise,
With pots full of dreams and mischievous lies.
Each new sprout's like a prank from a friend,
That laughs in the face of let's-not-pretend.

Diary of a Fertile Heart

Pages of green, I jot down its schemes,
Photosynthesis dreams and sunbeam extremes.
A plot twist here, a leaf that appears,
With every new sprout, I shed silly tears.

When watering day comes, it shouts with glee,
"Pour on, dear friend, I'm thirsty as can be!"
So, I dance with the can, like some mad ballet,
It wiggles and shakes, then sprays the café.

Glimpses of promise in each fuzzy leaf,
A heart full of laughter, and zero grief.
I scribble its quirks, document its stunts,
Between my mishaps and its tiny grunts.

Conversations on growth, a leafy tête-à-tête,
Delightful encounters, I'll never forget.
A plant with a penchant for fibs and for fun,
In this wacky diary, our tales will be spun.

The Leafy Letter

Dear friend of green, it's a pleasure to write,
Your leaves make my spirits soar, oh what a sight!
In this pot we dance, your roots wriggle with flair,
Don't leaf me alone, oh, please be aware!

Each new leaf unfurls, a joke in disguise,
I chuckle aloud at its shifty surprise.
Photosynthetic pranks, brightening my day,
In this veggie world, who needs dull play?

My green confidant, oh how you thrive,
In your company, I feel so alive.
You soak in the sun, I bask in your shine,
Together we giggle, a friendship divine.

So here's to our journey, you know I adore,
The duo of soil and sunlight galore.
May our leafy adventures never cease,
In this quirky tale, we harvest the peace.

Cultivated Dreams

In a pot of laughter, life takes its course,
Each sprout a charmer, with minimal force.
It reaches for sunlight, stretching so high,
Waving lush arms, saying, "Look at me fly!"

Tales of mishaps, I weave in my pot,
Moments of joy, each time it grows hot.
Repotted with love, it shrieks with delight,
A party of greens, oh what a sight!

Sunshine and water, a recipe grand,
But watch out for spills from this clumsy hand!
Soil on my shirt, I laugh with my plant,
We're quite the odd couple, a leafy savant.

So here's to the dreams nurtured in clay,
With laughter and fun leading the way.
A garden of goofballs, we sit side by side,
In this cultivated life, honor the ride!

A Journey in Verdant Hues

In a pot, so green and round,
A leafy friend I have found.
It never cries, it never pouts,
Just sits and watches while I shout.

Sunlight comes, a little too bright,
It's wearing shades, oh what a sight!
I water it just like a champ,
While it grows like a Green Giant lamp.

Each leaf a tale, each stem a jest,
Who knew that plants could be so blessed?
I tell it secrets, it nods in reply,
It's my chill buddy, oh my oh my!

With tiny pots and a dance of chance,
We share the space in a leafy dance.
I trip and stumble, it sways with glee,
Together we grow, just wait and see!

The Wisdom of Green Buds

With fingers crossed, I plant a seed,
Will it sprout? I hope indeed!
It leans to sunlight, takes a peek,
I laugh, it's playing hide and seek.

Leaves pointing up like tiny hands,
It waves good morning, makes no demands.
I whisper secrets, it listens close,
In green companionship, we both do boast.

It teaches patience, a lesson true,
Watch it grow, just like my shoe!
Each sprout a giggle, each thorn a tease,
I swear it knows my every sneeze.

Around the home, it starts to creep,
A plant that's funky, not too deep.
With every tendril, laughter grows,
In this leafy world, anything goes!

Nurturing Nature's Poems

I sprinkle soil like fairy dust,
With hopes and dreams, in plants I trust.
They sip on water, slurp like kids,
"Oh please," I say, "don't blow your lids!"

Tiny greens in pots of clay,
Turn day to dreams in a leafy play.
When I dance, they sway along
In rhythmic joy, they hum a song.

I talk to them as if they're wise,
Who knew green buds could tell no lies?
They nod and laugh, without a sound,
In our little world, true friendship found.

Each branch a joke, each leaf a pun,
Together we bask in the morning sun.
With giggles echoing through the air,
In this odd party, we are quite the pair!

Tendrils of Time

In the corner, a plant stands tall,
With tendrils stretching, it can't help but sprawl.
Every twist and turn tells a tale,
Of wild adventures, not one to fail.

It mocks my watering routine,
"Is that all you got?" it sings like a queen.
With each droplet, it paints the day,
In colors of green, in its playful sway.

Leaves winking as I walk by,
"Need some sun?" I hear it sigh.
Growing tall and full of jest,
A plant that knows I love it best.

In the chaos of life, it thrives and plays,
A little green joker in so many ways.
With roots in laughter, it climbs and blooms,
In this garden of life, no room for glooms.

The Collector of Green Dreams

In my home, green dreams reside,
Pot by pot, they're quite the guide.
One's a dancer, sways to the beat,
The other insists it's time for a tweet.

They chatter away, these leafy pets,
Sharing secrets, no need for bets.
They claim to know just how to grow,
But I'm the one who's down with the hoe.

Together we plot, under sun and shade,
Building a world where worries will fade.
I sing them songs, they hum right back,
A quirky band, on a green-tinted track.

So if you find your life's a bore,
Grab a pot or two—oh there's so much more!
You'll giggle and snort, that's guaranteed,
With these funny greens and their eccentric creed.

Nature's Gentle Reassurance

In the morning light, they greet the day,
Their cheerful faces chase gloom away.
One says, 'Hey, why the frown, old friend?'
Another pipes up, 'Let's just pretend!'

Their leaves hold tales from times gone by,
Of sunlight soaked in, oh my oh my!
They giggle softly when I confess,
My attempts to water are a messy process.

'More space, less stress!' is the leaf's advice,
But I just chuckle, 'Well, isn't that nice?'
With laughter they grow, that's the trick,
Who knew these greens could make life click?

So here we band, with roots entwined,
In a joyous dance that's one of a kind.
Nature whispers sweet, gentle laughs,
In this pot of green, we're the quirky crafts.

Insights from the Leafy Realm

In the corner, where the sunshine beams,
A council of green shares their dreams.
'Water me daily!' one leaf did shout,
While another chuckled, 'Doubt it, no doubt!'

They hold debates on the best sun spot,
While I ponder just where I forgot.
'Too much light!' cries one, while another snickers,
'More for me!' he says, as the plot thickens.

Each leaf has wisdom in silly disguise,
Like 'Watch the clouds, they'll make you wise!'
They tease me gently, but their roots stay deep,
In this leafy realm, we laugh and leap.

Thus, I note their quirks in my wild little book,
Esoteric wisdom—who knew I'd look?
In their leafy realm, absurdity reigns,
Through laughter I learn, it's joy that sustains.

Roots Under the Surface

Beneath the soil, secrets unfold,
Roots plot mischief, cunning and bold.
'Did you see that cat?' one whispers low,
'Trying to snack on us, oh no, oh no!'

They wiggle and giggle, teeter-totter,
Sharing tales of that naughty otter.
They swap stories, conspiratorial in tone,
With laughter that echoes, they're never alone.

Their roots intertwine like a wacky dance,
Each trying to outgrow the other's chance.
'Let's launch a garden party!' they say with glee,
'And invite the worms—they're quite the spree!'

So here's to roots, both stubborn and spry,
With humor they anchor, reaching for the sky.
They remind us that laughter, deep and profound,
Is the best way to grow in this crazy ground.

Vintage Pot Chronicles

In a pot so old, with cracks and stains,
A cactus moans, but still makes gains.
Water me, feed me, oh, what a song,
Yet here comes the cat, to prove me wrong.

With every sprout, it brings a tale,
Of resilience strong, just like a snail.
"Is this a plant or a quirky pet?"
It throws a leaf, and I just fret.

Colors fade, potted tales unfold,
A leafy laugh, the stories told.
From sunbaths warm to shadows drear,
My little buddies bring such cheer.

Oh, let them grow, they dance and sway,
One leaf whispers, "Hey, look my way!"
Vintage pots hold more than mere dirt,
A garden of giggles, never to hurt.

The Language of Leaves

A leaf leaned in, whispered with glee,
"Don't overwater, you'll drown me, you see!"
With such a chatty plant at my side,
I pondered their gossip, a leafy guide.

The succulents snicker, sharing their dreams,
"I hung out in sunlight, or so it seems!"
While ferns flip through pages of green,
Their soapy tangents, oddly serene.

"Tap-tap," said the twig, "knock knock! Who's there?"
A funny little sprout, waving with care.
In this garden of puns, plants have the knack,
To turn my frown into a laugh attack.

So I sit back and enjoy their taunts,
As sunlight glimmers on their sassy fronts.
With each new sprout comes a joke anew,
In the playful chatter, I find my crew.

Little Green Guardians

In pots lined up like brave little knights,
Guarding my desk from mundane sights.
"Fear not!" they shout, in eloquent glee,
"We'll battle stress, just wait and see!"

Green fingers wag, in comical fashion,
Tickling woes, they burst into laughter.
A succulent wink, a fern gives a shout,
"Who needs a therapist? We're all about!"

With leaves so bright and humor so loud,
They form a club, joyful and proud.
Guardians of giggles, with stories to share,
In this leafy fortress, I've found my heir.

They drink in sunshine, and spout out cheer,
While I am stuck with all of my fear.
Yet here they stand, my green squad so true,
Filling my life with their jests and their hue.

Serenity in a Terracotta Home

In a terracotta castle, plants hold court,
Silent observers at my own life sport.
"Did you see that?" the newbie sprout quips,
As I trip on a pot; now that's some slips!

A peace lily sighs, spreading calm through the air,
Boasting of roots, unaware of my care.
"Water me slowly, but give me some light!"
Each little guardian, a humorous sight.

The pots align like a quirky brigade,
Each with its tales that never will fade.
"Look at my color, isn't it grand?"
As they mock me gently, just like they planned.

In this home of terracotta, laughter prevails,
My leafy companions spin whimsical tales.
With every new leaf comes a chuckle and sigh,
In the realm of green, the worries pass by.

Earthly Meditations

In the pot sits a leafy friend,
Whispering secrets the roots can send.
A sip of sunlight, a splash of rain,
Chatting with greens, so blissfully plain.

Wobbly stems and a bit of a lean,
They've got style, like a fashion magazine.
What's their secret? Why, it's simple, you see,
Just stand there and bask, like a cup of tea!

Tiny pots, but the dreams are vast,
Sharing tales of the sunlit past.
Who needs therapy when you've got a leaf?
Nature's laughter, a joyful belief!

From the window, they grin and sway,
Sipping sunbeams all through the day.
Here's to the greens, the silly and spry,
Rooted in fun, reaching for the sky!

A Garden of Cultivated Thoughts

In a patch of dirt, wild ideas grow,
Thick as the clouds, flourishing slow.
A pot full of giggles, a sprinkle of glee,
Tending to laughter, oh how it can be!

What's that? A sprout with a cheeky grin?
Sharing its dreams, oh where to begin?
With a poke and a prod, they scheme and plot,
Who knew a cactus could be such a tot?

We water our worries with each gentle splash,
Sowing seeds of joy with a hearty dash.
What grows in the shade of our wittiest takes?
Why, a garden of thoughts that giggle and quake!

So grab your tools, let's dig in the fun,
With dirt on our hands, and smiles to stun.
For in every leaf, there's a story to tease,
Cultivated joy among the petals and breeze!

Moods in Green

There's a party in the pot, oh what a sight,
Dancing green leaves, oh what a delight!
A twist here, a turn there, just feeling so free,
Who knew a succulent could shimmy with glee?

When the sun starts to shine, they strike a pose,
Waving at passerby, in torn-up clothes.
They gossip with weeds, as if time stands still,
Flowering chaos, a riot of will!

"Oh be careful!" whispers a basil so sly,
"Watch out for snails, they're aiming to fly!"
With laughter that echoes through each leafy vein,
Who said that being green couldn't entertain?

So let's toast to moods, oh vibrant and keen,
In the tapestry woven, both wild and serene.
A garden's our stage, with nature's delight,
As pets of the earth, we sip joy's sweet bite!

Nature's Silent Embers

In the corner stands a sage-like sage,
Whispering wisdom with every stage.
A giggle escapes from a bushy mess,
Nature's confetti in this cozy denress.

Sipping on sunlight, what a tasty treat,
Who knew that soil could be such a feat?
In a world of chatter, they quietly bloom,
Creating a world from a little room!

The cacti wear hats, standing oh-so-tall,
While the ferns are gossiping—having a ball.
The sun's golden rays are the best kind of friends,
Warming them up as the laughter ascends.

So here's to the gentle, the silly, the keen,
In nature's embrace, our joy's evergreen.
In a troop of green buddies, we'll dance a jig,
For in quiet moments, life's heart gets big!

Planting Seeds of Reflection

In a pot so small and round,
A leafy friend I have found.
It stares and makes me question,
Is it clever or just a distraction?

Water it, but not too much,
Its thirst is subtle; not a touch.
Talk to it, give all the praise,
Or else it might put me in a haze!

In sunlight, it stretches wide,
Casting shadows, like it's trying to hide.
With every sprout, I feel a cheer,
Is it me or the plant that's unclear?

Each leaf is like a tiny smile,
Reminding me to take a while.
To ponder life, the funny bits,
And laugh with my little green sidekick.

The Green Heartbeat

In my room, a specter thrives,
With photosynthesis, it jives.
I swear it nods when I complain,
Green leaves flicking, mocking my pain!

It listens well, though leaves can't talk,
And judges me with every stalk.
Oh, the secrets it must keep,
While I spill all this emotional heap!

I dance around while it just stays,
Rooted deep in its calm ways.
Who's the silly one in this game?
I'm the clown and it's got no shame!

Sometimes I think it's plotting too,
To overthrow my funky crew.
But hey, if it grows stronger, that's fine,
As long as it shares some sun and wine!

Sheltered Under a Canopy

Beneath the leaves, I find my peace,
Watching tiny bugs release.
They frolic in a leafy dance,
While I stand back and take a chance!

With each new sprout, my worries fade,
I've become a plant parade!
They giggle as I tell my tales,
They're my audience—no more fails!

Shade provided, but watch your step,
A fallen leaf—what a misstep!
My friends, they join in on the fun,
In this foliage, we feel like one!

So here's to leaves both green and bold,
Sharing laughter, fortune told.
A strange crew, but quite a sight,
Beneath this canopy, joy takes flight!

Whispers of the Green Path

There's magic in the little things,
Like green leaves and what joy brings.
They rustle softly, share a joke,
If only I could hear each poke!

With every twist, they tell a tale,
Of sunlit days and rainy trails.
Their whispers tickle, make me grin,
While I ponder where I've been!

A gentle tug, oh watch your step!
Those are roots, not a trap, just prep!
Laughing, I stumble through their charm,
Embraced by greens, I feel no harm.

So join this path, where laughter prances,
Among the leaves, we take our chances.
In nature's jest, let's find delight,
With plants as friends, let spirits ignite!

Growth in Stillness

In a pot, I sit all day,
With thoughts that dance and play.
My leaves are wide, my roots are deep,
Yet still I can't find sleep.

Each moment's like a waiting game,
For sunlight's kiss, oh what a claim!
I stretch my stem, I wiggle bright,
Is it a plant or a silent fight?

Neighbors gossip, oh so sly,
'Look, she's growing—why? Oh why?'
I tease them with my still, green grace,
Plant envy written on their face.

With every inch, I chuckle with glee,
Who knew being rooted could be so free?
A leaf unfurls, a testament true,
To joys of patience and giggles anew.

Secrets of the Silken Stems

Whispers slither through the air,
In leaves that shine without a care.
Those silken stems hold tales so bold,
Of adventures in daylight and mysteries untold.

I caught a breeze—what did it say?
'You're a succulent star; let's play today!'
I giggle in leaf, I sway with delight,
Who knew being green could feel so right?

Watch me stretch, oh what a sight,
As I do the shimmy, much to your delight.
My friends around me sigh and pout,
While I'm the queen of this green house route.

Yes, I hold secrets, vibrant and smooth,
Of silly escapades and planty moves.
So if you dare, come sit and peep,
At the laughable tales my roots still keep.

The Untold Lives of Green

Amidst the soil, we play our roles,
With hidden dreams and daring goals.
Who knew a sprout could have such flair?
Or scheme beneath a garden chair?

I've seen the cats, their wild frolics,
Chasing shadows, oh such mock antics!
While I just sit, all calm and cool,
Mastering the art of the slow-and-smooth.

Our tales are brushed in hues of bright,
Some leafy gossip under the moonlight.
Daring plants from pots nearby,
Dream of adventures—oh, me oh my!

So if you think we just stand still,
Join our tea party, come share a thrill.
For in our hearts, the wild winds sing,
Of escapades and the joy we bring.

Echoes in Every Leaf

In emerald coats, we sway and sway,
Each leaf a note in nature's play.
Echoes of laughter on the breeze,
Tickle my veins, oh what a tease!

Oh, the pitter-patter of raindrops sweet,
Is like a dance beneath my feet.
As I shimmy and shake, I hear the sounds
Of whispers from my leafy crowns.

I might be rooted, but don't be fooled,
This plant has moves, I'm not just schooled!
With each new sprout, a story unfolds,
Of laughter, growth, and mysteries bold.

So next time you see me, take a pause,
In playful silence, let's give applause.
For in every leaf, there's joy to find,
An echo of giggles in nature intertwined.

Nature's Encrypted Blessings

In the corner, a green friend sits,
With leaves that chat like gossiping twits.
Water me, they beg, don't forget,
But only a drop, or I'll surely fret.

A nibble from critters, a taste test they hold,
Each leaf a fortune, or so I've been told.
Watch out, little bugs, you think you can stay?
I'm the pot gardener; you'll be on your way!

I talk to them softly, they seem to reply,
In shimmery whispers, they're such a sly tie.
They might be silent, but I know it's true,
They're plotting world takeovers, just me and you.

In the light, they shine like they own the room,
Bringing quirkiness, fun, with just a touch of gloom.
They thrive on my laughter, my wishes and dreams,
In this house of green mischief, nothing's as it seems.

Vignettes in Verdant Contrast

Oh, my leafy pals, you've got style and grace,
Sunbathing daily, each in your place.
One's always drooping, add a little cheer,
While another's growing wild, that's my dear!

When guests arrive, they give it a glance,
Thinking of leafy rebellion, a strange dance.
I swear they conspire behind every pot,
Plotting escape plans, a daring new plot.

Fertilizer jokes, they sure get a laugh,
Feeding each leaf, as if on a gaffe.
"Too much, too little!" we argue and fret,
But they thrive in chaos; it's a perfect duet.

In the sun's warm embrace, they shine like each star,
Making me wonder, just how weird we are.
Every leaf holds a secret, each petal a dream,
In this vibrant comedy, we're quite the team.

Beneath the Cocoon of Soil

In the muck of the earth, they wiggle and squirm,
Counting their blessings on each little germ.
Dirt is their wardrobe, their style is unique,
They treat every raindrop like a wild mystique.

Underneath, they scheme, beneath layers of clay,
Talking to roots in a most silly way.
"Where's our sunshine?" they grumble and pout,
While I just stand by, chuckling about.

Sprouts of green whisper, 'Is that a new leaf?'
Or maybe just rumors, much like a thief.
Each tiny bud has a tale to remark,
Of life in the soil, and dreams of the park.

So here's to my green friends, the quirkiest bunch,
With personalities that pack quite a punch.
They thrive in my chaos, they're living in jest,
And in this green kingdom, we're truly blessed.

Chronicles of a Green Enthusiast

I wake up each morning, with plants by my side,
They peek from their pots, full of leafy pride.
"Feed me today, oh master of fate!"
My green little buddies can hardly wait.

They chatter and giggle, I swear I can hear,
Amongst the fresh soil, there's laughter and cheer.
With pots as their thrones, they judge my attire,
This kingdom of leaves, my heartfelt desire.

Occasionally, I trip, spill water like rain,
And my leafy companions can't hide their disdain.
They shimmy and sway, pretending to mock,
In our little garden, it's quite the comical talk.

So I plant and I care, in this botanical spree,
With plants saying "You're stuck with us. Can't you see?"
In the saga of life that leaves me bemused,
It's a riot, this journey, oh how we're amused!

Stories from a Succulent Guardian

In my room, a tiny troop,
Green warriors in a potted loop.
They wiggle and wiggle, oh what a sight,
Taking over my desk by day and night.

Each leaf a letter, each stem a tale,
Of daring adventures in the sunlit gale.
Whispering secrets, they share with glee,
"Please water us, oh, can't you see?"

I tiptoe past with a grin so wide,
My leafy friends, they take it in stride.
They practice their poses, daydream in green,
The sassiest plants I ever have seen!

When I'm gone, they throw a wild feast,
A succulent soirée, to say the least.
Tiny pots dancing, oh what a show,
Just try and stop them! They put on a glow.

Echoes in the Soil

Down in the dirt, a chatter unfolds,
Tales of the pots and their winsome holds.
'Last week, I swear, I saw a worm,
It did a jig, and oh, how it squirmed!'

Soil friends share laughs, in colorful ranks,
'Can you believe those succulent pranks?'
'You think you're tough? Just check out my roots,
I've tangled with weeds and won in my boots!'

Fungi join in, with a laugh and a cheer,
'Let's talk about that time we held a seer!'
With spores in the air, they spin sweet lore,
'The rumors grow loud, oh, what's in store?'

As evening descends, the stories won't end,
In the cozy dark, the laughter transcends.
Each voice a reminder, both near and far,
Life in the soil shines like a star.

Reflections Through Thick Leaves

Peering through leaves, I spot my reflection,
A wild-haired gardener, in full perfection.
With dirt on my nose and a grin so wide,
These leafy pals take me in stride.

In morning sun, they hold their chat,
Discussing my flaws like a weathered old hat.
'How many times has he tripped on the rug?
Let's raise a leaf for that silly chug!'

Watering cans sing, as I dance on the floor,
While they roll their eyes—these greens want more!
Each droplet a tale in the laughter of light,
'Hydrate us, oh dear, it could be a fight!'

Evening falls, but who holds the key?
'We'll take over the world, just wait and see!'
In their thickly green wisdom, they plot and they scheme,
As I marvel at life, like a bone-tired dream.

Growing with Grace: A Green Memoir

Each day I ponder their growth and glee,
These little greens thrive with such esprit.
They dance in the sunlight, bask quite shameless,
Holding court in corners, oh, how they tame us!

'Curious humans,' they whisper and tease,
'A sprinkle of water, if you please!'
In the corner, a cactus gives side-eye with flair,
'Better watch out, I have spikes to spare!'

When I'm feeling blue, they cheer me right up,
With vibrant green whispers from each tiny cup.
Together we giggle at the days gone by,
In a world of mischief, our vibe won't die!

Thus, my life's memoirs are written in green,
Adventures galore, you've no idea what I mean!
With each tiny leaf, a story to tell,
I'll treasure these moments, oh, how they swell!

Garden of Resilience

In a pot I find my peace,
Leaves like laughter, never cease.
Sunshine beams, my leafy friend,
Wobbling tales that never end.

Water spills, they take a sip,
I trip over roots, a comic slip.
Each leaf a grin, with tales to share,
In this garden, love's in the air.

Fleeting moments, pots collide,
My green companions stand with pride.
With each new sprout, a giggle grows,
In nature's dance, the humor flows.

So here's to plants, a jolly crew,
With antics both green and brightly blue.
Their resilience makes my heart twirl,
In this funny, flourishing world.

Whispering Leaves

Little leaves, they wiggle and sway,
Whispering secrets in their own way.
They gossip 'bout sunshine, rain, and cheer,
In my cozy home, they persevere.

A phantom touch, I swear they're alive,
Cracking jokes while I barely survive.
In silent chuckles, they seem to say,
Just water us once—don't let us fray!

I dream of a party beneath the sun,
With snacks of soil, oh what fun!
Each leaf a guest with laughter loud,
In a soirée, vibrant and proud.

So here's to the whispers of green delight,
Doze off with plants, oh what a sight!
In this garden of giggles, joy's the theme,
As the world spins by, we live the dream.

Green Embrace

In my window, they do dance and prance,
With bouncy leaves, a silly romance.
They wiggle their roots, in soil they play,
Addressing the sun, they shout, 'Hip-hip- hooray!'

Every sprout tells tales of absurdity,
Like growing their hair in a wild flurry.
A tumble here; a spill there,
Oh dear, my green pals, handle with care!

With each fresh leaf, a smile will grow,
Our little party continues to flow.
Planting laughter in every nook,
Who knew that life could be this book?

So join this journey of leafy art,
In the clutches of green, we'll never part.
Embracing the quirks, let the good times roll,
In this fun and frolic, we find our soul.

Tales of Tender Succulents

In my humble nook, they sit quite proud,
Succulents smile, drawing a crowd.
Stories unfold with each little sip,
Of sunlight and love, they take a trip.

These plump little wonders, so round and sweet,
With humor they gather, oh what a feat!
In a gentle breeze, they sway and sway,
Grinning at life, come what may.

Stealing the light, they bask in glee,
While I sip my coffee, they tease me.
Their tales are silly, often absurd,
With insights expressed without a word.

So here's to the green, the quirky, the fine,
In their funny world, we intertwine.
Together we flourish, dance, and dive,
In this tapestry of green, we thrive!

Tales from the Verdant Sanctuary

In a pot with a grin, she stands tall,
Her leaves wear a crown, the queen of them all.
Neighbors stop by, they gossip and stare,
'Is it a plant? Or a pet? I declare!'

With water in hand, I play my part,
But she winks at me; I'm losing the start.
Overwater, and she sulks, grows a frown,
Underwater, she's the queen of the town!

I tell her my secrets, she sways with glee,
Keeps all my trials as green as a tree.
'Is it just me, or does time revamp?'
With joy in the air, she's quite the champ!

Each leaf is a story, a laugh to unfold,
In this verdant sanctuary, bright and bold.
With every sprout that dances in light,
Together we'll laugh into the night.

Leaves of Hope and History

In the kitchen, she's a silent muse,
Whispers of growth, in leafy hues.
Each leaf a story, a twist of fate,
"I'm here for the laughs, don't make me wait!"

A sprout of wisdom, she cheers me on,
"Water me well, or I might just yawn!"
Society tells me to 'Get things straight,'
But she just giggles, "Let's celebrate!"

Her roots dive deep, while I sip my tea,
She's a philosopher, always carefree.
Dancing in sunlight, a comic relief,
In my little haven, she brings true belief.

From tiny pots with personalities aplenty,
What's life without laughter? It's far too empty.
So here's to the leaves, both shiny and bright,
Together we flourish, a humorous sight!

Chronicles of a Plucky Green Friend

Once in a pot, a fellow so spry,
She raised her leaves, reaching for the sky.
'What's that, little buddy? The sun's in your eyes?'
A wise plant with humor, in her green disguise.

When chores feel heavy, she gives a cheer,
"Let's grow through this, my friend, have no fear!"
With each little leaf that dances in place,
A salute to resilience, a leafy embrace.

She teases my mornings, never too shy,
"Just one more drop, 'til I'm ready to fly!"
Laughing together, her spirit so free,
A buddy for life; it's just her and me.

Her branches stretch wide, like a belly that's full,
She keeps things light, it's the ultimate rule.
With courage unyielding, she helps me ascend,
In this journey of growth, she's my leafy friend!

The Botanic Diaries

Dear diary, I've met a new friend today,
With leaves that giggle and sway in the play.
'What's on the agenda?' she asks with a wink,
"Let's grow too tall, it'll really make them think!"

She thrives on my antics, this green little sprite,
With every new sprout, she brings pure delight.
"Watch out world, we're going outside!
These pot-bound worries, let's cast them aside!"

The morning sun greets us, both feeling so bright,
"Grab that watering can, let's make this right!"
With each splash of joy, we burst into fits,
An epic adventure, where laughter befits.

So here we remain, our stories collide,
In this pot of dreams, with humor as our guide.
Dear diary, let's see what tomorrow can bring,
With leaves and laughter, we'll take on the spring!

www.ingramcontent.com/pod-product-compliance
Lightning Source LLC
Chambersburg PA
CBHW070324120526
44590CB00017B/2809